Anyone making a change in their diet, especially if pregnant, infirm, elderly or under sixteen, should consult their GP. Dr Gillian McKeith is a Doctor of Philosophy in Nutrition (PhD), a qualification gained after several years of study from the American Holistic College of Nutrition, USA (now Clayton College). She is a postgraduate member of the Centre for Nutrition, UK. Before retraining in Nutrition, Gillian graduated with a BA from Edinburgh University, UK, and with an MA from the University of Pennsylvania, USA. Gillian has worked for over 15 years in the field of Nutrition. She is not a traditionally trained medical doctor.

MICHAEL JOSEPH
Published by the Penguin Group
Penguin Books Ltd, 80 Strand, London WC2R ORL, England
Penguin Group (USA) Inc., 375 Hudson Street, New York, New York 10014, USA
Penguin Group (Canada), 90 Eglinton Avenue East, Suite 700, Toronto, Ontario
Canada M4V 3B2
(a division of Pearson Penguin Canada Inc.)
Penguin Ireland, 25 St Stephen's Green, Dublin 2, Ireland
(a division of Penguin Books Ltd)
Penguin Group (Australia), 250 Camberwell Road,
Camberwell, Victoria 3124, Australia (a division of
Pearson Australia Group Pty Ltd)
Penguin Books India Pvt Ltd, 11 Community Centre,
Panchsheel Park, New Delhi - 110 017, India
Penguin Group (NZ), cnr Airborne and Rosedale Roads, Albany,
Auckland 1310, New Zealand (a division of Pearson New Zealand Ltd)
Penguin Books (South Africa) (Pty) Ltd, 24 Sturdee Avenue,
Rosebank, Johannesburg 2196, South Africa

Penguin Books Ltd, Registered Offices: 80 Strand, London WC2R ORL, England
www.penguin.com

First published 2006
1

Typeset by New Clarendon and Trade Gothic
Designed and typeset by Smith & Gilmour, London
Printed in Italy by Graphicom srl

A CIP catalogue record for this book is available from the British Library

ISBN-13: 978-0-718-14954-3
ISBN-10: X-0-718-14954-8

CONTENTS

Introduction 4

Shop Healthy 6

Reading Food Labels 11

Aisle by Aisle 17

Eating Out 88

Useful Lists 94

INTRODUCTION

If you've watched my television programme or read my books, you probably know by now about my passion for aduki beans. But where do I get them? You need to know this vital information, otherwise you might just miss out on my fabulous Aduki Bean Bake. Fret no more. To the rescue comes my new *Shopping Guide* briefing you on how to shop healthily, what to look for and where to find it.

Every food I want you to try is easily obtainable from the health food store or local supermarket. There's no need to fly to Tibet to hand pick antioxidant-packed Goji berries. You can actually buy them yards from the comfort of your own home.

So, it's now time to go beyond your comfort zone; push the envelope a wee bit when it comes to your food choices. Walk into a health food store even if it's for the first time. See what's in there. Explore aisles in the supermarket that you have never been down before.

I am on a mission to change this country's eating habits and I need your help to make that happen. I want to empower people to help themselves when it comes to their bodies and health. And that includes you. Food is one very powerful tool to help maintain a healthy body, mind and spirit. So knowledge about food is key.

Do not sit in the dark when it comes to what you can put into your body. Turn on your inner light, illuminate your path and visualize a healthy journey for life. Food is your fuel and there is an array of so many foods that many people I meet have never heard of, let alone have allowed to touch their lips.

Keep my new *Shopping Guide* in your kitchen, pop it in your handbag when you go out, slide it into the inside pocket of your jacket, sit it on your desk at the office or keep it in the car glove compartment. Have it handy at all times and take it with you to the shops. Dip in and out, use it like a dictionary, learn from it. This little guide can be your catalyst to reaching the pinnacle of health.

Love and Light

Gillian

www.drgillianmckeith.com

ONE
SHOP
HEALTHY

WHY SHOP HEALTHY?

As part of a healthy lifestyle, food can:

01 Lower the risk of heart disease, stroke, some cancers and other degenerative diseases

02 Improve your general sense of wellbeing and energy levels

03 Ease stress

04 Boost fertility

05 Help with mood swings

06 Improve skin, nails and hair vitality

07 Slow the ageing process

08 Strengthen your immune system

09 Help you sleep better

10 Ease headaches

GILLIAN'S TOP SHOPPING TIPS

》 Aim for the fresh food aisles first. You need to be eating at least five portions of vegetables and fruit every day, so stock up as often as possible! And being surrounded by all the colours and shapes of the fruit and veg will inspire you to seek out the best foods.

》 Go for variety. Don't buy the same foods every time you shop. See which fruit and veg are in season. Try out new herbs and spices. Ask the fishmonger what's freshest today. The key to a good diet is eating as many different types of healthy foods as possible, so be adventurous.

》 Whenever possible, choose the unprocessed, unrefined option. So that means brown rice instead of white, wholemeal bread instead of white sliced. And look carefully at the labels (see page 11 for details) to check for hidden nasties like added salt.

》 Steer your trolley clear of the junk foods. If there's an entire aisle stocked with crisps in your local store then simply skip it and move on.

» Never shop on an empty stomach. If you shop when hungry you'll head straight for junk foods to satisfy your sugar or salt cravings.

» Ask yourself which foods you feel like. Which herbs would you like to cook with this evening, which veggies look tempting? If you listen to your body and make intuitive food choices then you will make the right choices. Listen to your inner self.

» Visit your local health food store and you'll discover many new foods which might not yet be available in the supermarket. They are particularly good for offering a huge choice of herbal teas, miso products, tofu and tempeh and most types of grains, beans and pulses.

» Find out about local vegetable box schemes, which deliver directly to your home from a farm. One of the easiest ways to eat more veggies is to sign up for a box delivery scheme. Considering the convenience and the variety, you might be surprised at what good value many of these schemes are. Local produce is the freshest you can buy and the highest in nutritional value. It doesn't need to be sprayed with chemicals or vacuum sealed to keep it 'fresh' from farm to table. Organic vegetables with no pesticides are the best!

>> Get inspiration at your local market or farmer's market. If you have a market or farmer's market nearby then that's a fantastic way to get the whole family excited about food. Not only will you find out exactly what foods are freshest and in season, but there are often lots of opportunities to try out new flavours there and then. The more natural, unprocessed, real food you can include in your diet, the healthier it will be.

>> Before you shop it's a good idea to plan your meals for the days ahead and write a list. How are your cupboards looking on the ingredients front? Do you need to stock up on a few staples? If you need any healthy meal ideas then check out *Dr Gillian McKeith's Ultimate Health Plan* and my *You Are What You Eat Cookbook* for inspiration.

TWO
READING
FOOD
LABELS

HOW TO READ FOOD LABELS

Food labels are a great source of nutritional information, particularly when it comes to the nasties in food which you should try to avoid.

The ingredients are listed in descending order by weight, and include colour additives, preservatives, nutrients, fats or sugars which have been added. So if a food has sugar listed as the first ingredient, you know the sugar content is more than everything else.

MAIN INGREDIENTS TO KEEP LOW ON THE LIST

Salt

Most people eat far too much salt. For adults the recommendation is no more than 6g per day and for children see below (www.salt.gov.uk). When reading labels it's always a good idea to look for 'no added salt' if possible. Also be aware that if a label lists 'sodium' instead of 'salt' then 1g of sodium is roughly equivalent to 2.5g salt.

0–6 months less than 1g
7–12 months 1g
1–3 years 2g
4–6 years 3g
7–10 years 5g
11 years and over 6g

I always say that healthy foods, such as celery
and wakame, contain all the natural salt your
body needs, so if you eat a balanced diet you
don't need to add table salt to your meals.

Added sugar

Refined sugars are often added to food,
particularly soft drinks, biscuits, cakes, sweets,
most ready meals and some tinned foods. Avoid
added sugars where possible, and watch out for
these – they are all sugar under a different name:

>> Brown sugar
>> Cane juice
>> Corn sweetener
>> Corn syrup
>> Dextrose
>> Fructose
>> Glucose

>> High-fructose
>> Invert sugar
>> Lactose
>> Maltose
>> Raw cane sugar
>> Sucrose syrup

Look closely at the labels of 'low fat' foods as
they often contain high levels of sugar to make
up for the lack of flavour. Your body converts
excess sugar into bad fats anyway, so there's
really no benefit in substituting high levels
of sugar for low levels of fat.

Saturated fats

Saturated fats are found mainly in animal products, margarines, cooking fats, savoury and sweet snacks. Unfortunately, not all food labels differentiate between the saturated and unsaturated fat content. Try to get all your 'good' fats, the Essential Fatty Acids (sometimes called 'omegas'), from natural sources including avocados, oily fish, seeds and nuts, as well as olive, hemp and poppy oils.

Trans-fats

Trans-fats are produced when vegetable and fish oils are hydrogenated (chemically altered) to turn them into margarine or shortening. They are harmful to the body because they block the conversion of essential fats, and not only raise levels of bad blood cholesterol but lower levels of good. Low-fat spreads often contain hydrogenated or partially hydrogenated fats.

Additives and Preservatives

There are over 14,000 man-made substances added to our food supply today. It's important to be aware of the types of additives you could end up consuming if you are not careful. If you need a dictionary to decipher a food label, I'd say try and swap for something completely natural.

FOOD CLAIMS

Keep an eye out for food manufacturers' vague claims. For example, 'farm fresh' eggs will usually mean factory-farmed eggs (where hens are kept inside in wire cages called 'battery cages' stacked one on top of the other). The only terms which are regulated with eggs are 'organic' and 'free range', and these are the types that I prefer. The following terms may look appealing but are not regulated:

>> Natural
>> Lite
>> Traditional
>> Farm fresh
>> Low sugar
>> Low fat
>> 90% fat free!

TOP 10 FOOD ADDITIVES TO AVOID

01 Acesulfame-K

02 Artificial colourings

03 Aspartame

04 BHA and BHT

05 Caffeine

06 Monosodium Glutamate (MSG)

07 Nitrite and Nitrate

08 Potassium Bromate

09 Sulfites

10 Tartrazine

THREE
AISLE BY AISLE

Not every supermarket is the same, but they do tend to group certain foods together in a similar way. To make life easier for you, I've therefore arranged the food lists aisle by aisle. I've created a simple star sytem to help you choose: GREAT CHOICE means go for it and enjoy as much as you fancy, GOOD CHOICE means this is a healthy food but enjoy in moderation, OK means fine once in a while and AVOID means steer well clear! I have starred 30 of the foods in the charts that follow as my favourite 'super foods'. I've picked these because of their super abilities to boost health and vitality. Include these star super foods in your diet on a regular basis and you'll soon be on the path to a new you.

FRUIT

The key to healthy eating is variety, which includes fresh fruit. I would urge you not to get stuck in the rut of eating the same fruit every single day. It is much better than no fruit at all, mind you, but I still want to get tough with you on this point. The world has so much more to offer than oranges, which seem to be the only fruit many of the participants on my TV show eat when I first meet them. If you never eat berries, for example, then you will be missing out on the fantastic health properties of these super fruits.

Apple★ The old saying 'An apple a day keeps the doctor away' isn't just an old wives' tale. Apples contain the nutritional stars fibre and flavonoids, plus malic acid which helps digestion

Apricot, dried (see: Apricot, fresh)

Apricot, fresh Packed with vitamins A and C

Banana Good source of potassium, an essential mineral for maintaining normal blood pressure

Blackberries★ Abound in immune-boosting, anti-ageing antioxidants

Blackcurrants Rich in antioxidants and flavonoids, and decent source of vitamin C

Blueberries★ My favourite fruit, blueberries have many health benefits. One of the best

fruit sources of antioxidants, plus they are
anti-inflammatory, antibacterial and thought
to be anti-ageing

Cherries Traditionally used to treat gout

Coconut May help stabilize blood sugar levels

Cranberries May help reduce bladder infections

Currants, dried Antibacterial and anti-
inflammatory properties and may help
lower cholesterol

Damsons Rich in antioxidants and also
contain the amino acid tryptophan, which
is used by the body to produce the feel-good
neurotransmitter serotonin

Dates, dried (see: Dates, fresh)

Dates, fresh Fibre rich and energy boosting

Elderberries Source of anti-ageing antioxidants
and vitamins A, B and C

Figs, dried (see: Figs, fresh)

Figs, fresh Laxative properties and good
energy- boosting snack

Goji berries★ High berry source of antioxidants

Golden Inca berries★ Nutritional and
antioxidant powerhouse

Gooseberries Good source of vitamin C

Grapefruit, pink and white Packed with
immune-boosting vitamin C

Grapes, red and white Enhance liver function
and bile flow. Red grapes are good for the heart

and circulation

Greengages Antioxidants

Guava Vitamin C

Kiwi fruit Extremely nutritious

Kumquats Good source of fibre and vitamin C

Lemon★ The best start to the day is a cup of warm water with a squeeze of lemon juice. Lemons are rich in vitamin C and excellent for the digestion. You can even make lemon peel tea, as the peel has been found to have immune-enhancing properties

Lime Helps to destroy bad bacteria in the gut

Loganberries Antiviral and antibacterial

Loquats Rich in vitamin A and a good source of fibre

Lychees Good source of vitamin C and potassium

Mandarin Rich in antioxidants

Mango★ You have not lived if you haven't tried my mango and banana smoothie. I equate it to an internal deodorant. Its two key biochemical properties, anacardic acid and accardiol, are natural mood elevators

Melon, Cantaloupe Vitamin C and betacarotene

Melon, Galia Potassium and betacarotene

Melon, Honeydew Because of high water content it is a natural diuretic

Mulberries Contain pectin, which is good for cleansing the bowel, and malic acid, which can help improve energy

Nashi pears Rich in vitamin C as well as containing potassium and folate

Nectarines Rich in antioxidants

Oranges Source of bioflavonoids

Papaya (Paw-paw) Aids the digestive process

Passion fruit Contains antioxidants

Peach Gentle laxative effect

Pear Immune-boosting

Persimmon Prevents growth of bacteria in the intestines

Pineapple Digestive aid

Plantain May help to soothe the stomach and can strengthen the stomach lining as protection against ulcers

Plum Antioxidants

Pomegranate I use extracts of the fruit in cases of diminished libido

Prickly pear (Cactus fruit) Contains many flavonoids, including the anti-inflammatory quercetin

Prune Traditional remedy for constipation

Quince Improves digestion

Raspberries ★ If you want to pep up your sex

life then take a punnet of raspberries into the bedroom, because these are a great source of zinc, the sexy nutrient

Rhubarb Laxative effect

Satsuma Sweet, satisfying source of vitamin C

Sharon fruit Rich in vitamin A

Star fruit Good source of fibre and vitamin C

Strawberry Good source of antioxidants and zinc

Tamarind High in potassium

Tangerine A cup of hot water with tangerine peel is thought to aid digestion

Ugli fruit Comparable nutrition to citrus fruits

Watermelon★ High water content so good for cleansing the kidneys. If juicing watermelon, juice the rind too

RECIPE IDEAS

LEMON MOUSSE

SERVES 4
4 whole lemons
4 ripe avocados, stoned, peeled and mashed
juice of half a lemon
juice of half an orange
250g pitted dates
2 tbsp maple syrup
zest of 1 lemon

1 With a very sharp knife remove the skin from one of the lemons, leaving the body of the lemon whole. Cut in half and remove the seeds. Repeat for all the lemons.
2 Place all the ingredients, except the lemon zest, in a food processor and blend until smooth. Spoon into dessert dishes and chill for 2 hours in the fridge.
3 Serve garnished with lemon zest.

RHUBARB CRUMBLE

SERVES 2
100 g rhubarb, chopped
1/2 tbsp agave syrup
75 ml cold water
For the topping:
50 g porridge oats
1/2 tbsp millet flour
1 tbsp agave syrup

1 Place the rhubarb, agave syrup and water in a small pan. Cook over a gentle heat for 15 minutes.

2 Remove from the heat, allow to cool slightly and then transfer to a small pie dish.

3 Preheat the oven to 180C/gas mark 4.

4 Place the oats and flour in a mixing bowl and stir well. Then mix in the syrup. The mixture will appear a little lumpy.

5 Scatter the mixture over the fruit. Do not press the mixture down.

6 Transfer to the oven and bake for 15 minutes until the top is crisp.

7 Remove from the oven and allow to stand for 5 minutes before serving.

VEGETABLES

There is a huge array of vegetables to try. Choose what looks freshest and tastiest, and remember the more variety the healthier.

I have included a long list of vegtables on pages 28–29. Here are a few of my favourites with just a taste of their many health benefits:

Brassicas: Cabbage, cauliflower, kale, broccoli, Brussels sprouts, collard greens, mustard greens
Brassicas are a must have liver supporter in the diet. They contain ditholthiones, a group of powerful anti-carcinogenic compounds. Also present are isothiocyanate compounds such as sulforaphane which stimulate the body's defence against disease.

Dark green leafy greens: Kale, spinach, spring greens, watercress
More than 80% of the people who come to see me for the first time test deficient in one or more major minerals of the body. To get more minerals, you must eat lots of dark leafy greens in your diet. They are a rich source of vitamins, minerals and phytochemicals which help support the liver.

Root vegetables: Sweet potato, yam, parsnip, turnip

These vegetables are packed with nutrition, flavour and disease-fighting nutrients. Root vegetables are recommended for diabetics, as they convert sugar into energy slowly and steadily. For example, sweet potatoes have been found to stabilize blood sugar levels because of their carotenoid content.

Alliums: Onion, leek, garlic

One of garlic's star ingredients is allicin, a sulphur compound which is produced when the cloves are crushed. Not only does it give garlic its pungent smell, but it also has several beneficial health effects, including the ability to lower blood pressure as well as levels of triglycerides and cholesterol in the blood, and to kill bad bacteria and viruses.

Onions are a good source of quercetin, a flavonol which has anti-carcinogenic properties. It has been found that the stronger the onion, the greater the concentration of antioxidant and anti-carcinogenic compounds.

Pumpkins and squash

Squash can be eaten raw or cooked. Summer squashes contain a lot of water, fibre, betacarotene, are cooling and have diuretic qualities. I like to make raw squash spaghetti. Pumpkin can help to balance blood sugar levels due to slow energy release. Squash seeds and pumpkin seeds are also beneficial for destroying intestinal worms. Courgettes or zucchini are a type of summer squash. They are one of the best plant sources of lutein and zeaxanthin, two carotenoids which are essential for good eye health.

Edible stems: Asparagus, celery, fennel, kohlrabi

Edible stems tend to have a good water content so are good for juicing. They contain magnesium, potassium and folic acid as well as being a good source of fibre. They are also low in fat and calories. Asparagus is a source of glutathione, an important antioxidant and cell protector. It also contains rutin, which helps protect blood vessels.

GREAT CHOICE ★ ★ ★

>> Artichoke, Globe
>> Artichoke, Jerusalem
>> Asparagus ★
>> Aubergine
>> Avocado ★
>> Beet greens
>> Beetroot
>> Bok choy
>> Broccoli ★
>> Brussels sprouts
>> Carrots
>> Cauliflower
>> Celeriac
>> Celery
>> Chard
>> Chicory
>> Chinese leaves
>> Collard greens
>> Courgette
>> Cucumber
>> Daikon
>> Dandelion flowers
>> Dandelion greens
>> Endive
>> Escarole
>> Fennel
>> Green beans
>> Green cabbage
>> Green peas
>> Haikido squash
>> Kale
>> Kohlrabi

>> Leeks
>> Lettuce, Cos
>> Lettuce, Iceberg
>> Lettuce, Lamb's
>> Lettuce, Little Gem
>> Lettuce, Romaine
>> Mangetout peas
>> Marrow
>> Mushrooms
   (Shiitake are my favourite ★)
>> Mustard greens/cress
>> Okra
>> Olives
>> Onion
>> Onion squash
>> Parsnips
>> Peppers, green, red,
   orange and yellow
>> Purple sprouting broccoli
>> Radicchio
>> Radishes
>> Red cabbage
>> Rocket
>> Salsify
>> Sauerkraut
>> Savoy cabbage
>> Shallots
>> Sorrell
>> Spinach
>> Spring greens
>> Spring onions
>> Squash, Acorn

›› Squash, Butternut
›› Sugarsnap peas
›› Swede
›› Sweetcorn
›› Swiss chard ★
›› Tomatoes
›› Turnip
›› Turnip greens
›› Watercress ★
›› White Cabbage
›› Yams

OK ★

›› White potatoes (can cause a sugar rush, so eat with beans or legumes such as lentils, and no more than once a week)

Handy hint 🛒

Don't boil your vegetables to death. Steam them for a few minutes or eat them raw wherever possible.

RECIPE IDEAS

ASPARAGUS RISOTTO

SERVES 4

1 bunch fresh asparagus
1 leek, halved and thinly sliced, reserve
the trimmings
1 ltr water
1 bay leaf
2 cloves garlic, peeled
1 tsp olive oil
2 tbsp water (for water frying)
300 g short grain brown rice
2 tbsp flat leaf parsley
1 tbsp lemon juice
1 handful fresh rocket

1 Take the asparagus spears and snap the tough
base from the stem. The asparagus will naturally
break at the best point. Chop the asparagus into
1.5cm pieces.

2 Place the leek trimmings and the discarded
asparagus bases in a medium-sized pan, pour in
the water and bring to the boil. Add the bay leaf
and leave to simmer.

3 In a non-stick frying pan heat the oil with 2 tbsp
water and add the sliced leek and garlic. Cook
for 5 minutes to soften but not colour, then spoon
in 2 tbsp of the asparagus water from the
simmering pan.

4 Add the rice and cook for a few minutes, stirring continuously. Add 200 ml of the simmering asparagus water, cook for a few minutes until the rice absorbs all the water and then add a further 200 ml of asparagus water.

5 Continue to add the hot asparagus liquid to the rice and cook over a gentle heat for approximately 30 minutes. The rice should require about 800 ml of liquid. Discard the leek and asparagus trimmings.

6 Add the chopped asparagus to the rice, stir well and simmer for a further 5 minutes. Add the parsley and lemon juice. If required, add a little more stock. The rice should be tender and moist.

7 Serve the risotto in warmed soup plates and scatter with the fresh rocket.

CHINESE CABBAGE CASSEROLE

SERVES 4

1 ltr water
1 2cm piece fresh ginger, sliced
1 tsp coriander seeds, crushed
1 clove garlic, peeled
600g Chinese cabbage
100g Daikon (or radish), peeled
and cut into julienne or matchsticks
100g carrots, peeled and sliced
4 tbsp fresh coriander, chopped
1 tsp sesame oil
1 tsp wheat-free soy sauce
1 tbsp sesame seeds
20g arame soaked in cold water
for 10 minutes and drained

1 Place the water, ginger, coriander seeds and garlic in a medium to large saucepan. Bring to the boil.
2 Add the cabbage, Daikon and carrot and simmer for 5 minutes.
3 Remove from the heat and stir in half the coriander.
4 Spoon into soup bowls and drizzle over the oil, soy sauce, sesame seeds, remaining coriander and arame. Serve.

FRESH HERBS

Herbs are powerful super foods that contain a wide range of nutrients and provide you with some of nature's very best flavours. Keep a few pots of basil, coriander, parsley or mint on your kitchen window sill. The delicious scents and rich colours will be sure to fire up your passion for healthy eating. Don't be shy when it comes to cooking with herbs – you won't miss salt when you throw in handfuls of herbs. Most major supermarkets now stock a fantastic array of fresh herbs (see page 63 for dried herbs). Garden centres will often offer an extensive choice of potted herbs and seeds for your garden or patio. Herbs have extensive therapeutic properties. In fact, much of the research into conventional medicine originates from the healing powers of plant properties.

Basil Good for digestion
Bay leaves Aromatic (remember not to actually eat the leaves)
Chervil Eases digestion
Chives Can help with hypertension, and rich in vitamin C and iron
Coriander Assists with the absorption of nutrients

Dill High in fibre, iron, magnesium and calcium

Garlic ★ May help with high blood pressure, heart health, reducing bad bacteria and fighting viruses

Ginger Can be helpful to combat nausea and vomiting, colds and flu

Lovage A diuretic, so useful with any weight loss programme

Marjoram A good source of energy-boosting iron

Mint Relieves intestinal gas

Oregano Antioxidant (antioxidants are powerful allies in helping to prevent cancer, heart disease and stroke)

Parsley ★ A nutrient powerhouse, including betacarotene, calcium and more vitamin C than citrus fruits

Rosemary Beneficial for the immune system and also thought to improve memory and concentration

Sage May ease menopausal symptoms

Sorrel Immune system nourisher

Tarragon A source of magnesium

Thyme Antiseptic properties and respiratory aid

RAW NUTS AND SEEDS

Look for naked nuts only. In other words, unsalted, raw and sugar-free. These are often found with the fruit and veg.

NUTS – GOOD CHOICE ★★

Almonds★ High in antioxidants and may help lower cholesterol

Brazil nuts Richest of all nuts in selenium, which is a natural mood lifter

Cashews Good source of a variety of nutrients and protein

Chestnuts A rich source of good omega fats (don't eat chestnuts raw)

Coconut High in protein and good fats

Hazelnuts★ Rich in vitamin E, for anti-ageing and antioxidant properties

Pecans Contain plant sterols which help prevent heart disease and lower cholesterol

Pistachios Good for the intestines, liver and immune system

Walnuts High in Omega 3 essential fatty acids and so very heart healthy

OK ★

Peanuts Some people are allergic to peanuts; the symptoms include vomiting and diarrhoea

AVOID ✖

All roasted or salted nuts

SEEDS – GREAT CHOICE ★ ★ ★

Flax One of the best plant sources of Omega 3 essential fatty acids, beneficial for general health and vitality

Hemp seeds★ Rich source of essential fatty acids and protein. Best to eat raw and shelled

Pine nuts Laxative properties

Poppy Good source of calcium, magnesium and essential fatty acids

Pumpkin★ Good source of the libido-boosting mineral zinc and eaten regularly, pumpkin seeds can rid the intestinal tract of unwanted parasites

Sesame Packed with B vitamins

Sunflower Source of vitamin E, for improving your skin's radiance

SPROUTED SEEDS – GREAT CHOICE ★ ★ ★

Alfalfa★ Good source of food enzymes, which enhance digestion and absorption of nutrients and may also help in the breakdown of fat

Beansprouts Packed with protein and food enzymes and helpful for liver function

Clover All sprouts are beneficial for digestion, nutrient absorption and raised levels of energy

RECIPE IDEA 🍴

CASHEW TOFU SALAD

SERVES 2

1 tbsp olive oil
1 red pepper, cut into 2cm pieces
75g mangetout, trimmed
1 tsp wheat-free tamari sauce
75g firm tofu, cut into small squares
2 spring onions, trimmed and sliced
10g plain cashew nuts, roughly chopped
1 romaine lettuce heart, leaves separated,
washed and drained
extra virgin olive oil and tamari sauce,
to serve

1 Heat the oil in a large wok with a little
water. Sauté the pepper over a medium heat
for 2 minutes.
2 Add the mangetout and sauté for 30 seconds.
Remove from the heat and sprinkle with the
tamari sauce.
3 Arrange the lettuce leaves in two bowls – tearing
in half first if the leaves are large. Scatter the
pepper and mangetout over the lettuce.
4 Arrange tofu squares on top. Sprinkle with
the spring onions and nuts.
5 Drizzle with a little olive oil and extra tamari
sauce to serve.

FISH AND SHELLFISH

Freshwater and oily fish are rich in the good fats, known as omega 3, essential for reducing cholesterol and promoting health and vitality. They are also low in saturated fat. Ask the fishmonger what he recommends as the freshest that day and choose wild rather than farmed where possible.

GREAT CHOICE ★ ★ ★

>> Carp
>> Cod *nucless*
>> Dover sole
>> Flounder
>> Haddock
>> Hake
>> Halibut
>> John Dory
>> Kipper
>> Lemon sole
>> Mackerel
>> Monkfish

>> Pilchards
>> Plaice
>> Polack
>> Red mullet *Triglia*
>> Salmon ★
>> Sardines
>> Sea bass *browns*
>> Sea bream
>> Snapper
>> Swordfish
>> Trout
>> Whitebait

AVOID ✖

>> Anchovies
>> Crab
>> Herring
>> Lobster
>> Mussels
>> Oysters
>> Prawns
>> Scallops
>> Scampi
>> Squid
>> All fried fish

RECIPE IDEAS 🍴

POACHED MONKFISH WITH TARRAGON

SERVES 2

140 g baby spinach leaves
2 vine-ripened tomatoes, sliced
500 ml water
1 bay leaf
1–2 cm piece fresh ginger, peeled
1 lemongrass stalk
2 cloves garlic, peeled
1 Kaffir lime leaf, or juice of lime
1 tsp fresh miso paste
200 g piece fresh monkfish
large handful fresh tarragon
1 tsp olive oil

1 Arrange the baby spinach and tomatoes on a serving plate.
2 Bring the water to the boil with the bay leaf, ginger, lemongrass, garlic, Kaffir lime leaf and miso paste. Boil for 5 minutes and then reduce to a simmer.
3 Poach the fish for 3–4 minutes or until firm to the touch.
4 Remove the fish from the pan and keep it warm while you finish the sauce.
5 Boil the liquid until the volume has reduced by half.

6 Remove from the heat and strain into a small bowl, discarding the flavouring.

7 Add the tarragon and oil, and with a hand-held blender blitz until smooth. Alternatively this can be done in a small processor.

8 Place the fish on the spinach and tomatoes, spoon over the sauce and serve.

BAKED SALMON WITH SPINACH AND LEEKS

SERVES 4

2 leeks, washed, trimmed and sliced
500 g fresh baby spinach leaves
4 x 100 g organic salmon fillets
1 tbsp olive oil
2 garlic cloves, peeled and finely chopped
1 tbsp grated fresh root ginger
juice of half a lemon
1 handful fresh coriander leaves, to garnish

1 Preheat the oven to 200C/gas mark 6.

2 Gently boil or steam the leeks for 5 minutes to soften.

3 Place the spinach leaves in a medium-sized baking tin and top with the leeks. Place the salmon on the top.

4 Mix together the oil, garlic and ginger and liberally brush over the salmon using a pastry brush. Pour over the lemon juice.

5 Place in the oven and bake for 10 minutes. Remove and allow to rest for 5 minutes. Garnish with fresh coriander leaves.

MEAT, POULTRY AND GAME

If you want to include meat in your diet then
I recommend you buy free range, organic, or talk
to your local butcher about the leaner options.

GOOD CHOICE ★★
>> Chicken (skinless)
>> Turkey (skinless)

OK ★
>> Guinea fowl
>> Pheasant
>> Rabbit
>> Venison

AVOID ✖
>> Bacon
>> Beef
>> Duck
>> Gammon
>> Ham
>> Kidney
>> Lamb
>> Liver
>> Pork
>> Salami
>> Sausage
>> Veal

RECIPE IDEAS 🍴

POACHED CHICKEN IN GINGER MISO

SERVES 1

1 organic chicken breast
300 ml vegetable stock or make stock
with a veggie cube
1 tbsp organic miso
1–2 cm piece of fresh ginger
2 cloves garlic, peeled and chopped
3 tbsp fresh coriander
1/2 red pepper, finely sliced
1 handful beansprouts
2 bok choy trimmed and roughly chopped,
save 2 leaves for garnish

1 Preheat oven to 200C/gas mark 6. Take a large
sheet of foil and place the chicken in the centre.
2 In a small pan, bring the stock to the boil
and add the miso, ginger, garlic and 1 tbsp of
the coriander.
3 Form the foil into a bowl shape and spoon the
flavoured stock over the chicken. Scrunch the
foil up to create a parcel. Transfer to a baking
tray and cook for 10 minutes.
4 Arrange the bok choy on a serving plate.
Transfer the cooked chicken on to the bok choy
and then sprinkle over the pepper and sprouts.
5 Garnish with the 2 whole leaves of bok choy
and remaining coriander. Serve immediately.

WARM CHICKEN SALAD

SERVES 2

2 skinless organic chicken breasts
75 g green beans, trimmed
75 g asparagus spears
6 cherry tomatoes, halved
2 tbsp pine nuts
4 tbsp chopped fresh basil
1 handful baby salad leaves

DRESSING:

2 tbsp extra virgin olive oil
1 tsp cider vinegar
1 tsp Dijon mustard

1 Place the chicken in a small pan of cold water,
bring to the boil, then lower the heat and simmer
for 8–10 minutes. Remove from the pan and allow
to cool slightly. Alternatively, steam the chicken.

2 Steam the green beans and asparagus spears
until tender; refresh in cold water.

3 Mix the beans and asparagus with all the other
salad ingredients in a bowl except for the baby
salad leaves.

4 Place the dressing ingredients in a screw-top
jar with 1 tablespoon of water and shake well.

5 Slice the chicken while still warm and add to
the salad. Pour over the dressing and toss to coat.

6 Serve in a large salad bowl, garnished with
the baby salad leaves.

SOYA (TOFU, TEMPEH)

GOOD CHOICE ★★

Soya contains all the essential amino acids as well as some fibre. It is low in fat and contains phytoestrogens that can help balance female hormones. Processed soya products such as textured vegetable protein (TVP) are not recommended as they contain salt and flavourings. Avoid products that use soya isolates. Soya can be allergenic for some people and those with an underactive thyroid should limit their intake as it can be goitregenic (can suppress thyroid function). Use of sea vegetables with soya can reduce this effect. Soya may not be suitable for children under the age of 5 due to its hormonal effect, and many soya products are GM (genetically modified) so look out for this and buy organic where possible. Check out hemp sauce as an alternative to soy sauce for flavouring dishes.

RECIPE IDEA 🍴

ROOT VEGETABLES AND TOFU EN PAPILLOTTE

SERVES 4

2 tsp olive oil
2 carrots, trimmed, peeled and cut into
fine julienne (matchstick) strips
1 parsnip, trimmed, peeled and cut into
fine julienne strips
2 sweet potatoes, peeled and cut into fine
julienne strips
2 courgettes, trimmed and cut into fine
julienne strips
225g block smoked tofu, cut into 2cm cubes
1 tsp ground cumin
2 tsp tamari sauce
4 tsp freshly pressed apple juice
4 bay leaves
2 tbsp sesame seeds
4 tbsp fresh beansprouts

1 Preheat the oven to 200C/gas mark 6.
2 Take 4 pieces of foil, 30cm square, and brush
the centre of each with a little oil.
3 Mix all the vegetables together in a large bowl
and divide between the foil sheets.
4 Place the tofu on top of the vegetables. Season
with the cumin and bring the foil up around the
vegetables to form a parcel. Add the tamari and
apple juice and top with a bay leaf. Add a little
water to each parcel and then scrunch up the
foil to seal everything in.

5 Transfer to the oven and bake for 20 minutes.
6 Remove from the oven and allow to stand for
5 minutes. Transfer the foil parcels to serving
plates. Open up the parcels slightly and sprinkle
on the sesame seeds and sprouts and serve
immediately.

DAIRY

Many people are intolerant to dairy products as they contain hard to digest sugars and proteins. I have lost count of the number of people who tell me they feel better when they give dairy a wide berth. (If you really must drink cow's milk, then boil it first to make it more digestible.)
Goat's and sheep's products can be easier to digest. And fermented products such as yoghurt and kefir are easier to deal with as they are partially digested by the beneficial bacteria they contain. These bacteria are great for gut health and immune function. But if you are going to opt for a yoghurt, make sure that it does not have added sugar or sweeteners.

Organic products are recommended so as to avoid antibiotic and hormone residues that may be present in conventional products. Organic dairy products are also often higher in the healthy omega fats.

GOOD CHOICE ★ ★
➤➤ Organic goat's yoghurt
➤➤ Natural, organic unsweetened yoghurt

OK ★
>> Goat's milk
>> Goat's cheese
>> Greek feta cheese
>> Soft cheeses

AVOID ✖
>> Buffalo mozzarella
>> Butter
>> Cow's milk
>> Cream
>> Cream cheese
>> Crème fraîche
>> Fromage frais
>> Hard cheeses

EGGS

Eggs are a good source of usable protein as well as many vitamins, minerals and lecithin, important for the brain and nerve function. Eggs may be allergenic for some and hard to digest for some people. Always choose organic or free range.

RECIPE IDEA 🍴

GOAT'S CHEESE SALAD

SERVES 4

4 red peppers, deseeded and halved
12 cherry tomatoes
2 tsp olive oil
125g goat's cheese, crumbled
2 tbsp pine nuts
200g rocket
2 tbsp chopped fresh basil

1 Preheat the oven to 200C/gas mark 6.
2 Place the peppers (cut side up) and tomatoes
on a baking tray, drizzle with olive oil and roast
for 10 minutes. Sprinkle the goat's cheese inside
the peppers and cook for a further 5 minutes.
3 Scatter over the pine nuts and return to the
oven for 5 more minutes.
4 Arrange the rocket on 4 plates, top with the
peppers and tomatoes. Serve garnished with
the fresh basil.

FRESH SOUPS

I love soups. They can be so nutritious and easy
to digest. I always prefer you make your own soups
whenever possible for maximum healthiness and
taste. I find it almost therapeutic; softening some
onion, steaming a few carrots, tossing in some
chopped ginger or a handful of coriander and then
blitzing in a blender with some vegetable stock.
Many pre-prepared soups will have added cream
or salt when it's really not necessary. Lots of
homemade soups have a lovely creamy texture
with no need for added cream. Below I've listed
some of my favourite soup ingredients, and also
a quick checklist of added ingredients to avoid
if you have to resort to pre-prepared.

FAVOURITE SOUPS

>> Carrot and Coriander
>> Carrot and Ginger
>> Broccoli and Almond
>> Leek and Courgette
>> Beetroot and Celery
>> Butternut Squash
>> White Bean
>> Pea and Mint
>> Tomato and Basil

>> Miso and Shiitake Mushroom
>> Spinach and Nutmeg
>> Kale and Spinach
>> Lettuce (yes, really! See my
   You Are What You Eat Cookbook)
>> Fennel and Leek
>> Cauliflower and Cumin
>> Split Pea and Lentil

GREAT CHOICE SOUP ADDITIONS ★ ★ ★
>> Chopped nuts
>> Seeds
>> Sprouted seeds
>> Brown rice
>> Pearl barley
>> Pressed hemp or flax seed oils
>> Fresh herbs

BAD SOUP ADDITIONS ✖
>> Salt
>> Sugar
>> Cheese
>> Cow's milk
>> Cream

FRESH DIPS

Below I've listed my favourite homemade dip combinations; simply whizz them up in a food processor. Unfortunately the dips and spreads you might find ready made can contain hidden nasties, so I've added a few quick tips when searching for healthy pre-prepared options.

HOME-MADE COMBINATIONS

» Butternut squash, sesame seeds, brown miso paste

» Butternut squash, miso paste, fresh root ginger, lemon zest

» Butter beans, garlic, olive oil, parsley, lemon juice

» Cashew nuts (soaked overnight), tamari sauce

» Almonds (soaked overnight), pine nuts, lemon juice, olive oil, fresh basil

» Black olives (pitted), garlic, lemon juice

» Avocado, spring onion, garlic, fresh coriander, lime juice (homemade guacamole)

» Chickpeas, garlic, tahini, lemon juice, olive oil, fresh coriander (homemade hummus)

» Tomato (cooked), garlic, red onion, fresh basil

» Natural yoghurt, fresh chives, fresh mint

OK ★

>> Shop-bought hummus can be a healthy option
>> Yoghurt-based dips are a healthier alternative to sour cream
>> No-added-sugar salsas (mild)

AVOID ✖

>> Liver paté
>> Taramasalata

CHILLED JUICES AND SMOOTHIES

Look for freshly squeezed and freshly pressed juices, made from 100% vegetables or fruit. I also recommend you avoid the dairy-based smoothies – it's best to eat, or in this case drink fruit separately from other foods, for better digestion. Ideally, you should juice or blend your own fresh vegetables or fruit, but some ready-made options are still a healthy way to boost your fruit and veg intake. I am a big fan of pure veggie juices – you'll feel great if you drink these.

I'm a bit of a smoothie nut too. When making your own, you can throw in anything which takes your fancy. Add a little pressed apple juice or water if you find them a bit thick. Here are a few of my favourites to get you started:

>> Raspberries, mango and banana
>> Nectarine, apricot and pineapple
>> Freshly squeezed pink grapefruit juice
>> Simply strawberries and banana
>> Blueberries, blackberries and banana
>> Cranberries, raspberries and freshly pressed pear juice
>> Strawberries, peach and banana
>> Pears, peach and apple
>> Create your own masterpiece and enjoy!

CHILLED READY MEALS

Many of the conventional microwavable ready meals are simply not good for you. Often, they are loaded with added sugar, salt and a cocktail of chemicals. Having said that, not all ready meals are bad, so if you're short of time and looking for a pre-packaged meal, check the labels to make sure you've chosen the healthiest option available.

FROZEN FOODS

People often think that there can't be anything healthy in the frozen food section. Check out these frozen food standbys when in a pinch.

GOOD CHOICE ★★
>> Berries
>> Fish fillets
>> Peas
>> Corn
>> Broccoli

AVOID ✖
>> Cakes
>> Ice cream
>> Pizzas
>> Most ready meals
>> Sausages

OK ★
>> Natural unsweetened frozen yoghurt

GRAINS, RICE, PASTA AND NOODLES

Grains are a fantastic source of slow-release energy. The most important thing to remember when shopping for grains is to go for unrefined grains, for example white rice is refined and brown rice is unrefined. Not every grain I list here will be available in your supermarket, but the good news is that the choice does seem to be increasing fast. Try your local health food shop for some of the lesser-known grains. They all have individual textures and tastes, so it's worth branching out.

Grains are not only a source of good carbohydrates, but also fibre, B vitamins, vitamin E, calcium, magnesium, potassium, iron, zinc, copper and selenium. A healthy diet rich in unrefined grains has been shown to help lower cholesterol and regulate blood sugar levels. Eating a wide variety can also be helpful in preventing food allergies or intolerances.

GREAT CHOICE ★ ★ ★

>> Amaranth
>> Barley
>> Brown rice ★
>> Buckwheat
>> Bulgar wheat
>> Kamut
>> Millet
>> Oats
>> Pearl barley
>> Quinoa ★
>> Rye
>> Spelt
>> Teff

OK ★

>> Basmati rice
>> Brown rice noodles
>> Corn
>> Couscous
>> Polenta
>> Red rice
>> Rice pasta
>> Risotto (arborio) rice
>> Semolina
>> Spelt pasta
>> Wheat-free pasta
>> Wholemeal pasta
>> Wild rice

AVOID ✖

>> Egg noodles
>> White pasta
>> White rice
>> White rice noodles

Handy hints 🛒

Make sure you cook your grains until tender but firm. Chew them well for good digestion. It is best to store your grains in sealed containers. You can even keep them in the fridge or freezer for maximum freshness. My favourite ways to enjoy grains are as accompaniments to bean dishes, as breakfast porridges or mixed in with a salad.

RECIPE IDEAS

BUCKWHEAT CINNAMON PORRIDGE

SERVES 1-2

125g buckwheat groats
1 tsp lemon zest and a squeeze of lemon juice
1/2 tsp of peeled and grated fresh ginger
1 cinnamon stick, broken
sunflower seeds

1 Place the buckwheat, lemon zest and juice, ginger, cinnamon and 500 ml of water in a pan. Bring to the boil, then lower the heat and simmer for approximately 20 minutes.
2 Serve with a sprinkle of sunflower seeds.

BARLEY SOUP

SERVES 1

4 tbsp pearl barley
(soaked in cold water overnight)
2 sachets white miso
4 shiitake mushrooms

1 Drain the barley.
2 Bring 125 ml water to the boil and add the barley.
3 Bring back to the boil, then lower the heat and simmer for 10 minutes.
4 Add the white miso and shiitake mushrooms, simmer for a further 5 minutes and then serve.

DRIED BEANS AND PULSES

Beans are rich in essential nutrients, high in fibre and are a source of healthy omega fats. They are the perfect choice if you want to lose weight. Beans are an excellent source of protein and a diet rich in these foods can help lower cholesterol and the risk of heart attack. In general, when you eat beans and grains together a complete protein is formed, which the body can easily absorb.

GREAT CHOICE ★ ★ ★

>> Aduki ★
>> Black bean
>> Black-eyed pea
>> Broad (fava) bean
>> Butter bean
>> Cannellini
>> Chickpea
>> Flageolet
>> Haricot
>> Kidney
>> Lentil
>> Mung bean ★
>> Soy bean
>> Split pea

RECIPE IDEAS 🍴

ADUKI BEAN BAKE

SERVES 2

1 tbsp olive oil, plus extra for brushing
1 medium onion, peeled and chopped
2 garlic cloves, peeled and crushed
1 small squash, peeled and diced
1 large carrot, peeled and diced
1 celery stick, trimmed and sliced
500ml just-boiled water
1 tsp organic vegetable bouillon
(stock) powder
165g cooked aduki beans
1 medium leek, trimmed and sliced
2 tsp cornflour or arrowroot blended with
1 tbsp cold water to make a smooth paste
1 large sweet potato, cut into 5mm slices
(if you like a lot of topping, use 2 potatoes)

1 Heat the oil in a large saucepan with a tiny bit
of water, so you are water sautéing really. You
are not frying in the normal sense of the word.
2 Gently water sauté the onion and garlic for
3 minutes, stirring occasionally.
3 Add the squash, carrot and celery. Cook with the
onion and garlic for 2 minutes, stirring regularly.
4 Pour the just-boiled water over the vegetables
and stir in the bouillon powder.
5 Bring to the boil, then reduce the heat and
simmer for 10 minutes.

6 Preheat the oven to 200C/Gas 6.

7 Stir the sliced leek and aduki beans into the vegetable mixture. Return to a simmer and cook for 5 minutes, stirring occasionally.

8 Add the cornflour or arrowroot mixture and cook for about 1 minute, stirring until the sauce thickens.

9 Remove from the heat and transfer carefully into a 900ml ovenproof dish.

10 Arrange slices of the sweet potato on top of the bean and vegetable mixture. Brush with a little of the oil and bake for about 30 minutes until the potato is soft.

11 Serve with freshly cooked Savoy cabbage, green beans or broccoli and raw mangetout.

SPLIT PEA SOUP

SERVES 4

225 g yellow split peas, presoaked for
12 hours or overnight in cold water
1 wheat-free vegetable stock cube
1 tsp wheat-free vegetable bouillon powder
1 onion, peeled and sliced
1 sweet potato, peeled and chopped
3 carrots, trimmed, peeled and thickly sliced
4 sprigs fresh mint
4 handfuls fresh baby spinach leaves

1 Place the presoaked peas in a sieve and rinse
well in cold water. Transfer to a large saucepan
and cover with 1.5 litres cold water, the stock cube
and the bouillon powder. Bring to the boil, then
lower the heat and simmer for 25 minutes. Remove
any scum that rises to the surface with a spoon.

2 Add all the other vegetables and simmer for
a further 15–20 minutes or until the vegetables
are tender when pierced with a knife.

3 Remove from the heat and allow to cool, then
blend the soup in a food processor or with a hand-
held blender until smooth.

4 Return to the pan and re-heat, stirring gently.
Divide between warmed soup bowls, garnish
with the fresh mint. Add the raw spinach leaves
before serving.

DRIED HERBS AND SPICES

Add herbs and gentle spices to your salads, soups and stews for full flavour. You won't need salt.

>> Agar
>> Allspice
>> Aniseed
>> Bay leaves
>> Cardamom
>> Cayenne
>> Celery seeds
>> Cinnamon
>> Cloves
>> Coriander
>> Cumin
>> Fenugreek
>> Mace
>> Mustard seeds
>> Nutmeg
>> Oregano
>> Saffron
>> Star anise
>> Tarragon
>> Thyme
>> Turmeric
>> Vanilla pods

RECIPE IDEA

VANILLA AND CINNAMON RICE PUDDING

SERVES 1

350ml water or rice milk
100g organic short grain brown rice
1/4 stick cinnamon
1/4 pod vanilla
zest and juice of 1/2 orange
1 tbsp agave syrup (if you use rice milk,
you won't need the agave)

1 Place the water or rice milk in a small saucepan,
add the rice, cinnamon, vanilla, orange zest and
juice and the syrup if using.
2 Bring to the boil, cover and simmer for 25–30
minutes, stirring occasionally.

CONDIMENTS, OILS AND VINEGARS

Your store-cupboard ingredients are a good way to add interesting flavours to your dishes, but always look carefully at the labels of the following foods for signs of added sugar, salt or unhealthy fats.

GOOD CHOICE ★ ★

Black onion seed Salt substitute
Bouillon, vegetable
Harissa
Miso paste or powder★
Mustard
Peppercorns, black or green (Don't use too much pepper as it can be an irritant)
Sea salt (see page 12 for daily intake)
Savoury herb Salt substitute
Sushi ginger
Tahini
Tamari (soy sauce)
Umeboshi plum sauce
Vinegar, brown rice
Vinegar, cider
Vinegar, red wine
Vinegar, Umeboshi
Vinegar, white wine
Wasabi paste

OILS – GOOD CHOICE ★★

Avocado Rich source of good fats

Hemp Perfect ratio of essential fatty acids
and a complete protein

Olive★ High in monounsaturated fatty acids,
helps reduce blood cholesterol levels

Poppy seed oil High in omegas and minerals

Pumpkin High in essential fatty acids
and minerals

Sesame Increases energy

Sunflower Source of vitamin E

Walnut Good source of essential fatty acids,
minerals and protein

AVOID ✖

>> Mayonnaise

>> Salad dressings

>> Sauces – brown and tomato (there are now tomato sauces
available with no added sugar or salt – these are fine)

>> Table salt

RECIPE IDEA

HERBY SALAD DRESSING

MAKES 130ML,
KEEPS FOR 3 DAYS IN THE FRIDGE
8 tbsp olive oil
2 tbsp cider vinegar
1 tsp Dijon mustard
half a garlic clove, peeled and chopped
1 tbsp chopped fresh herbs
1/4 tsp wheat-free vegetable bouillon powder

Place all the ingredients, together with 2 tbsp of cold water, in a small screw-top jar and shake well.

Handy hint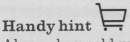
Always buy cold-pressed nut and seed oils.

TINNED PULSES, BEANS AND VEGETABLES

Always make sure there is no added sugar or salt in your tinned foods. Pulses and beans are often either in brine or water, so be careful to go for the water options.

GOOD CHOICE ★★
>> Baked beans
>> Beans
    Broad
    Butter
    Flageolet
    Haricot
    Kidney
>> Chick peas
>> Pulses
    Green lentils
    Red lentils
    Split peas
>> Sweetcorn
>> Tomatoes
    Passata
    Paste
    Tinned

AVOID ✖
>> Carrots
>> Fruit
>> Peas

TINNED FISH

Grilling fresh fish is quick, easy and healthy. Sometimes you may want an alternative option and tinned fish is fine on occasion. Go for fish which is tinned in water and look for dolphin friendly tuna.

GOOD CHOICE ★ ★
>> Mackerel fillets (in water)
>> Pilchards (in water)
>> Salmon (in water)
>> Sardines (in water)
>> Tuna (in water)

OK ★
>> As above in sunflower or olive oil
>> Sardines in tomato sauce

AVOID ✖
>> All fish canned in salt/brine
>> Anchovies

RECIPE IDEA

TUNA NIÇOISE

SERVES 4

1 tin tuna, drained
1 bunch asparagus tips
4 baby gem lettuces
200 g baby spinach leaves
2 tbsp black olives
150 g cherry tomatoes, halved
2 hard-boiled eggs, shelled and cut in quarters
(optional)
DRESSING:
1 tsp Dijon mustard
1 tbsp olive oil
2 tsp cider vinegar

1 Break up the tuna into chunks.
2 Bring a small pan of water to the boil, add the asparagus and cook for 2 minutes. Remove from the heat, drain and refresh in plenty of cold water.
3 Arrange the lettuce leaves, spinach, olives, tomatoes and asparagus tips on a platter. Scatter the tuna chunks over the leaves. Add the egg if using.
4 For the dressing, mix the mustard with 1 tsp of water, then whisk in the oil and vinegar. Drizzle over the salad and serve.

BREAD AND OTHER BAKED GOODS

Always choose whole-grain options when it comes
to breads and other baked products. Grains are
a great source of slow-releasing energy, when
in whole-grain unrefined form. But white grain
products are not good – giving you a rollercoaster
of highs and lows and the dreaded afternoon
slump. While whole-grain wheat is fine on
occasion, as a population we tend to eat too much
wheat. Look out for breads made from other
grains for variety. If you suffer from irritable
bowel syndrome then you will need to cut out
wheat altogether, and candida sufferers need to
steer clear of foods containing yeast.

GOOD CHOICE ★ ★

>> Granary bread
>> Oat cakes
>> Rice cakes
>> Rye bread
>> Wheat-free breads
>> Wheatgerm
>> Wholemeal/seeded breads
>> Wholemeal pitta
>> Wholemeal tortilla

AVOID ✖

>> Doughnuts
>> Fruit pies
>> Meat pies and pasties
>> Pastries
>> Pizza
>> Pork pies
>> Quiche
>> Sausage rolls
>> Scones
>> Sponge cakes
>> Sweet biscuits
>> White breads

RECIPE IDEA

GILLIAN'S SQUASH BREAD

MAKES 1 ROUND 12-CM LOAF
1 small butternut squash
300 g wholemeal flour
2 tsp baking powder
1 tsp herbal seasoning (optional)
2 tbsp olive oil

1 Preheat the oven to 200C/gas mark 6.
Place the whole butternut squash on a baking
tray and bake for 45 minutes or until very soft.
Cool on the tray for 30 minutes.

2 Carefully peel the skin from the squash and cut
away the stalk. Transfer to a large bowl and break
open using a spoon. Scoop out and discard any
seeds. Mash well with a potato masher. Measure
out 375 g of the squash and place in a large bowl.

3 Add the flour, baking powder and seasoning, if
using. Stir in 65 ml cold water and the olive oil and
mix together with a large spoon. Place on a lightly
floured surface and knead until soft and spongy.
Add a little more flour if the mixture is too sticky.
Form into a round loaf 12 cm in diameter.

4 Place on a lightly oiled baking tray and make
a cross on the top with a sharp knife. Bake in
the oven for 30–35 minutes.

5 Remove from the oven and, using oven gloves, carefully turn the bread over and tap the base gently. It should sound hollow. If it doesn't, return to the oven and cook for a further 5 minutes. Serve the bread warm or cold.

Handy hint 🛒

Many people have developed a sensitivity to the gluten in wheat. If you are intolerant to gluten then there are a number of wheat- and gluten-free breads available in health food shops and supermarkets.

BREAKFAST CEREALS

I say 'Breakfast like a king' and you'll be on the right path to a healthy diet. But you need to be careful when choosing cereals because so many have hidden sugar, even muesli. But nothing beats a bowl of porridge in the morning for keeping you energized and on the go throughout the day.

GREAT CHOICE ★ ★ ★
>> Amaranth flakes
>> Bran
>> Kamut berries
>> Millet flakes
>> Muesli (no added sugar)
>> Porridge oats
>> Spelt

OK ★
>> Cornflakes (no added sugar)
>> Puffed rice (no added sugar)

AVOID ✖
>> Cereals with added sugar
>> Fruity cereal bars with added sugar
>> Granola with added sugar
>> Muesli with added sugar
>> Puffed wheat with added sugar

FLOURS

You won't need all of these flours all of the time, but they do show how many interesting alternatives there are.

GREAT CHOICE ★ ★ ★

>> Amaranth flour
>> Buckwheat flour
>> Chickpea flour
>> Gram flour
>> Lentil flour
>> Millet flour
>> Oat flour
>> Potato flour
>> Quinoa flour
>> Rice flour
>> Rye flour
>> Soy flour
>> Spelt flour
>> Sunflower seed flour
>> Tapioca flour
>> Wholewheat flour
>> Yellow corn flour

AVOID ✖

>> Refined white flour

JAM, HONEY AND SWEETENERS

There are a number of natural sweeteners which are fine to use in moderation. Avoid all types of white refined, cane or brown. Refined sugar has no nutritional value and sweet products are often packed with calories, additives, colourings and preservatives.

GOOD CHOICE ★ ★
>> Agave syrup
>> Almond extract
>> Apple juice (pure)
>> Barley malt extract
>> Brown rice syrup
>> Carob amazake
>> Grape juice (pure)
>> Malt extract
>> Mirin
>> Molasses
>> Vanilla extract

OK ★
>> Honey
>> Maple syrup
>> No-added-sugar jams

AVOID ✖
>> Added-sugar jams and jellies
>> All artificial sugar substitutes
>> All sugar
>> Corn syrups

RECIPE IDEA

BAKED APPLES WITH RAISIN COMPOTE

SERVES 4
**4 cooking apples, cored and halved
horizontally
2 tbsp raisins
2 tbsp sultanas
2 tbsp maple syrup or agave syrup**

1 Preheat the over to 200C/gas mark 6. Place
the apples in an ovenproof baking dish.
Mix the raisins and sultanas together and
stuff them into the holes left by the apple cores.
Drizzle a little syrup into each apple.
2 Bake for 15–20 minutes and serve warm.

SNACKS

Here are some snack ideas from your local supermarket, plus a few extra ideas you can easily and quickly prepare at home.

GREAT CHOICE ★ ★ ★
Nuts Check these are unroasted and unsalted, raw options. They might be easier to find in the fresh produce aisle (see page 35).

OK ★
Rice crackers Check for unhealthy additives like salt and artificial flavourings. You can find healthy seaweed rice crackers in health food shops.
Fruit and nut mixes

AVOID ✖
>> Bombay mix
>> Chocolate
>> Crisps
>> Flavoured nuts (smoked, for example)
>> Roasted nuts
>> Salted nuts

ALTERNATIVE SNACK IDEAS

Oatcakes and hummus

Raw vegetable crudités and dips (see page 53)

A piece of fresh fruit

A handful of seeds or nuts

Toasted nori strips – you can buy these in
health food shops

Baked veggies – bake slices of beetroot, squash,
pumpkin or parsnip for approximately 25 minutes
for a delicious hot snack

RECIPE IDEA

CRISPY KALE

SERVES 4
olive oil
100 g curly kale, stems removed
1 tsp dried mixed herbs

1 Preheat the oven to 180C/gas mark 4. Line a baking tray with foil and lightly brush with a little olive oil using a pastry brush.
2 Cut the leaves into wide slices and arrange evenly spaced on the baking tray.
3 Bake for 15–20 minutes, being sure to stir them at least twice while they're baking. The kale leaves are ready when they're bright green and crisp.
4 Remove the leaves from the oven and season with dried mixed herbs. Eat on the same day.

DRINKS

Water★ is by far the best thirst quencher and vitality booster. Lack of water can slow the body's metabolic rate and cause headaches, poor concentration and fatigue. Drink about eight glasses every day for ultimate wellness. When choosing fruit juices, cordials or energy drinks, always make sure there is no added sugar or artificial sweeteners.

TEAS
Herbal teas are a wonderfully healthy drink option. There's a vast array of choices available so give them a try and find your favourites.

Borage May help with easing symptoms of irritable bowel syndrome

Camomile Calming

Dandelion Cleansing to the liver and is a natural diuretic, so helpful in weight loss and fluid retention

Fennel Tummy soother

Fresh mint Eases digestion

Ginger Improves digestion and circulation and wards off colds and flu

Ginseng May help adrenal glands

Green Contains antioxidants (but also some caffeine)

Hawthorn Heart healthy

Horsetail Rejuvenating for nails and hair

Lemon balm Mood-lifter and nerve-soother

Linden flower Calming for inducing sleep

Liquorice Improves digestion

Melissa Calms nerves and eases indigestion

Mullein Clears mucous

Nettle★ Cleansing and detoxifying. Nettle root is also being used in the treatment of enlarged prostate

Pau d'Arco Antibacterial and antifungal, so can help sufferers with yeast problems, digestive disorders and general immunity (frequent colds)

Peppermint Soothing for digestion

Raspberry Prenatal tone-up

Red clover Antioxidant

Rosehip High in vitamin C

Sage Can ease sore throats. Can also help to reduce hot flushes in menopause

Slippery elm A natural anti-inflammatory which can soothe stomach, bowels and urinary tract

Spearmint Digestion

Valerian root Known for its calming effect to help induce sleep

ADVANCED HEALTH FOODS

Many great superfoods, which may originally have only been stocked in health food stores, are now available in some supermarkets. I recommend trying the following:

Algae and Spirulina
Algae is high in nutrients and easily digested, can strengthen your immunity and improve your memory. I like the liquid form best as it is easily digested and absorbed. Spirulina is high in protein and may help control blood sugar and cravings.

Aloe vera
Useful for digestive disorders, bloating, gas and flatulence. Drinking 1/4 cup before meals may help relieve these symptoms. You may want to mix this with fruit juice for a pleasant taste.

Amaranth
Contains calcium, magnesium and a host of other minerals. Makes for the perfect breakfast cereal or as a side dish.

Astragalus
An all-round energy- and immune-helper to fight colds and flu.

Goji berries

Discovered in the Himalayas, these berries are high in antioxidants. They contain an array of trace minerals, amino acids and are loaded with vitamin C. They are an amazing power food and so delicious too!

Hemp seeds

These contain a perfect ratio of essential fatty acids (omegas) and protein. I call this my weight-loss seed. Just be sure to get them shelled and raw.

Kamut

Many wheat-sensitive people tolerate kamut. It contains essential fatty acids, twice as much protein as wheat, and more minerals.

Miso

Miso is fermented soybeans, which you can find in paste or powder form. There are many varieties, from light to dark, and it's a good source of B vitamins. Use it to make soups, sauces, dips and to flavour any dish or stir-fry.

Quinoa

This South American seed is becoming widely available and contains all the essential amino acids for complete usable protein.

Royal jelly and bee pollen

Royal jelly is helpful for energy and combating stress. Bee pollen is a powerhouse of nutrients and can be used to fight chronic infections, nutritional deficiencies and allergies such as hayfever.

Sea vegetables

Seaweeds generally contain more minerals than any other food source. Some different types include dulse, nori, wakame, kombu and arame.

Siberian ginseng

A rejuvenative herb that helps the body adapt to stress. Beneficial to patients during or after illness and just after surgery for its restorative and anti-infection qualities.

Spelt

This grain is strengthening to the constitutional organs. It stimulates the immune system and can help constipation, colitis and poor digestion.

Sprouting seeds

Seeds like alfalfa, clover, broccoli and mung can be used to sprout baby shoots. Sprouted seeds are high in antioxidants and are packed with vitamins, minerals, protein and fibre as well

as two anti-ageing constituents – RNA and DNA –
that are only found in living cells.

Teff

A tiny seed with lots of flavour. It is high in
protein, with proper levels of calcium,
magnesium and iron. Teff is a good choice for
people who crave salt.

Tofu and Tempeh

Tofu is made from soya beans and is high in
protein and calcium. It can also help lower
cholesterol levels. Tempeh is a great meat
alternative.

Wheat grass

The actual wheat grass is virtually indigestible
so it needs to be juiced. There are many health
benefits: it is restorative to the endocrine and
immune systems.

TOP TEN

GILLIAN'S TOP TEN SUPPLEMENTS

01 Multivitamin

02 Liquid algae or green superfood

03 Milk thistle

04 Digestive enzyme supplement

05 Flax seed oil, hemp seed oil or starflower oil

06 B complex

07 Astragalus

08 Co enzyme q 10

09 Aloe vera juice

10 Probiotics

FOUR
EATING
OUT

Variety is your ally when eating out. For example, if you often buy your lunch out, don't settle for the same old sandwich and crisps. Nowadays, most eateries offer wide selections of salads, soups, vegetables, veggie casseroles and more.

Make sure you have healthy snacks on hand during the day. A handful of nuts or seeds, a piece of fruit or some veggie crudités are all perfect snacks.

AVOID

SNACK NASTIES

01 Crisps

02 Chocolate bars

03 Sweets

04 Cake

05 Biscuits

06 Salted nuts

07 Fizzy drink (regular or diet)

Handy hint
Drink a glass of water 20 minutes
before you eat. This will help you
feel fuller and will help digestion.

SANDWICH AND SNACK BARS

❯❯ Try to avoid dairy cream-based soups. But generally, soups are a great option when eating out.

❯❯ Look carefully at juices and smoothies. Try to buy freshly pressed, squeezed or blended fruit.

❯❯ Salads are a great option, but make sure they are not drenched in high-fat, high-calorie dressings.

❯❯ Sushi is an option, but not every day as I wouldn't recommend you eat too much white rice. Check out my *Ultimate Health Plan* for a brown rice sushi wrap recipe.

Handy hint 🛒
Always try to eat some raw veggies with your lunch or dinner. A side salad is a fine accompaniment.

RESTAURANTS

BRITISH

Traditional British cooking can be very healthy, but often isn't. The best option is to keep things simple. So instead of battered fish and chips, go for grilled fish with spring vegetables. And look out for hidden ingredients, particularly butter and cream. Ask for the gravy, sauce or dressing to be served on the side so that you can decide how much you want.

ITALIAN

The Mediterranean diet is rich in good fats such as olive oil and in vegetables, especially tomatoes. But typical British-Italian fare is often less healthy; thicker-based pizzas with lots of cheese on top and large pasta portions (Italians tend to eat a small amount of pasta as a starter). But you can have a very healthy meal in an Italian restaurant. For example, a big green herby salad to start with a drizzle of olive oil, followed by tomato-sauce-based pasta or fish.

FRENCH

You do have to watch out for butter and cream in many French dishes, so steer clear of these ingredients and stick to simple dishes with lots of steamed side vegetables. This is the healthy route.

INDIAN AND THAI

In India, food is traditionally incredibly healthy because it's a mainly vegetarian-based diet with simple, herb- and spice-rich sauces. However, in the UK, Indian food is often quite rich and yet again overloaded with cream and butter. Overly spicy food can be an irritant to the digestive system. A mild vegetable curry is a good option, with simple side dishes like sag (spinach) or dahl (lentils). In Thai restaurants, avoid battered or fried starters, but a simple green curry is a great choice.

CHINESE

Always check whether a Chinese restaurant uses MSG in its cooking. Monosodium glutamate is an addictive additive which can make many people feel very strange. But many Chinese restaurants now cook without MSG, so it's always a good idea to ask them to hold the MSG! Choose vegetable dishes where possible, steamed rice, and don't touch anything deep fried.

JAPANESE

Japanese food includes lots of my healthy staples, for example tofu, fish, sea vegetables, green tea, miso, shiitake mushrooms, lots of vegetables and sprouts. My favourite restaurant is Japanese as these foods can be so healing.

VEGETARIAN

You might think all vegetarian foods must be healthy for you. This isn't always the case. I've seen vegetarians live on junk foods like crisps, pizza and sweets. Watch out for overuse of ingredients like cheese, and ask how the food is cooked. Grilled or baked food is always preferable to fried. I don't mind stir-fries but ask that the chef use a very small amount of oil, and that it's one of the cold-pressed healthy oils (see page 66). At home make sure you water fry. This means using oil and water together, which is a much healthier option. Lots of vegetarian dishes are wonderfully healthy, though, so if you have a restaurant or café near you which serves vegetarian fare then I say go for it.

FIVE USEFUL LISTS

FOODS TO CALM THE STOMACH

>> Apples
>> Artichokes
>> Brown rice
>> Carrots
>> Fennel
>> Ginger
>> Sprouted seeds
>> Parsnips
>> Squash
>> Sweet potatoes
>> Tofu
>> Turnips
>> Yams
>> Teas/herbs: Fennel, peppermint, liquorice

FOODS TO EASE STRESS

>> Soaked almonds
>> Asparagus
>> Avocados
>> Berries
>> Brown rice
>> Cabbage
>> Celery
>> Garlic
>> Seeds

FOODS TO FIGHT COLDS AND FLU

- Astragalus
- Echinacea
- Ginger
- Goji berries
- Lemon
- Liquorice root
- Olive leaf
- Oregon grape
- Pau d'Arco tea
- Reishi and shiitake mushrooms
- Sprouted broccoli seeds

FOODS TO BOOST YOUR SEX DRIVE

- Aduki beans
- Asparagus
- Bananas
- Beetroot
- Berries
- Brazil nuts
- Fennel
- Figs
- Ginger
- Hemp seeds (raw shelled)
- Nutmeg
- Oats
- Parsley
- Pomegranates
- Pumpkin
- Saffron
- Sauerkraut
- Seeds
- Strawberries
- Vanilla

FOODS FOR ENERGY

- Asparagus
- Broccoli
- Flax seeds
- Goji berries
- Grains
- Grapes
- Mung beans
- Oats
- Parsley
- Peaches
- Seaweed
- Spinach
- Sprouts
- Sunflower seeds
- Wheat grass
- Yams and squashes